Product Manager Product Success:

How to keep your product on track and make it become a success

I0472437

"Practical, proven techniques that will help you to make your product management job a success"

Dr. Jim Anderson

Published by:

Blue Elephant Consulting

Tampa, Florida

Printed in the United States of America

Library of Congress Control Number: 2013916651

ISBN-13: 978-1492380160
ISBN-10: 1492380164

Warning – Disclaimer

Acknowledgements

Any book like this one is the result of years of real-world work experience. In my over 25 years of working for 7 different firms, I have met countless fantastic people and I've been mentored by some truly exceptional ones. Although I've probably forgotten some of the people who made me the person that I am today, here is my attempt to finally give them the recognition that they so truly deserve:

- Thomas P. Anderson
- Art Puett
- Bobbi Marshall
- Bob Boggs

Dr. Jim Anderson

This book is dedicated to my wife Lori. None of this would have been possible without her love and support.

Thanks for the best 21 years of my life (so far)...!

Blue
Elephant
Consulting

Speaking.   Negotiating.   Managing.   Marketing.

Table Of Contents

What's The Best Way To Start?

Congratulations — you are a product manager. Or you want to be one. No matter where your career is at right now, what we need to have a talk about is how you can take it to the next level.

Being a product manager is a strange sort of job. It turns out that you don't actually "do" anything. Instead, it's your job to get a lot of other people to do all of the things that are going to be required in order to make a product or a group of products be successful.

Needless to say this is a hard thing to do. However, as hard as that is, there is something else that you need to be doing at the same time: managing your career. Look, the success of your product is never only in your hands. Market conditions, what your competition does, and the whims of your customers will all conspire to either make your product a success or a flop.

No matter what the final result is, and often we don't even get to stick around for the last chapter, you are going to want your efforts today to move your career forward tomorrow.

What this means for you is that you need to understand what it is going to take to get the rest of your company to recognize the good work that you are doing today and the potential that you have for tomorrow. The good news is that this can be easily done. You just have to know how.

Product managers can get caught up in the details of their product. There always seem to be new requirements to create, product launches to schedule, and features to document. However, the secret to being a successful product manager is to realize that the job is really about having good communication skills. It's the people that you work with both inside of your company as well as outside of your company that will determine how far you'll go in your career.

This book has been written to give you a helping hand. I want to get you to take notice of the day-to-day things that are going to play a role in determining the next step in your career. It's not going to be your technical knowledge or your understanding of your market that is going to help you to move to the next level, but rather how others perceive you.

Contained in this book are the tips and tricks that you are going to need in order to take control of your product manager career. As you read each chapter, take a moment to think about how you can start to use the information in your job immediately. I think that you are going to be both surprised and pleased with just how much this information is going to help you take your product manager career to the next level!

Good luck!

-    Dr. Jim Anderson, October, 2013

About The Author

I must confess that I never set out to be a product manager. When I went to school, I studied Computer Science and thought that I'd get a nice job programming and that would be that. Well, at least part of that plan worked out!

My first job was working for Boeing on their F/A-18 fighter jet program. I spent my days programming fighter jet software in assembly language and I loved it. The U.S. government decided to save some money and went looking for other countries to sell this plane to. This put me into an unfamiliar role: I started to meet with foreign military officials in order to explain what my product did.

Time moved on and so did I. I found myself working for Siemens, the big German telecommunications company. They were making phone switches and selling them to the seven U.S. phone companies. The problem was that the switches were too complicated. Customers couldn't tell the difference between one complicated phone switch from another complicated phone switch.

The Siemens sales folks were in a bind. They didn't know enough about how the switches worked to tell their customers why they should buy them. Siemens reached out into their engineering unit looking for anyone who could help the sales teams out. I put my hand up and overnight I became a product manager.

Since then I've spent over 20 years working as a product manager for both big companies and startups. This has given me an opportunity to do everything that a product manager does many, many times. I know what works as well as what doesn't work.

I now live in Tampa Florida where I spend my time managing my consulting business, Blue Elephant Consulting, teaching college courses at the University of South Florida, and traveling to work with companies like yours to share the knowledge that I have about how product managers can make their product be a success.

I'm always available to answer questions and I can be reached at:

Dr. Jim Anderson
Blue Elephant Consulting
Email: jim@BlueElephantConsulting.com
Facebook: http://goo.gl/1TVoK
Web: http://www.BlueElephantConsulting.com/

"Unforgettable communication skills that will set your ideas free..."

Create Products Your Customers Want At A Price That They Are Willing To Pay!

Dr. Jim Anderson is available to provide training and coaching on the two topics that are the most important to product managers everywhere: how do I create the products that my customers want and what should I price them at?

Dr. Anderson believes that in order to both learn and remember what he says, product managers need to laugh. Each one of his speeches is full of fun and humor so that what he says "sticks" with everyone.

Dr. Anderson's Product Management Training Includes:

1. How can you segment your market?
2. What problems are your customers having right now?
3. Which of your customer's problems does your product solve?
4. How much of this problem does your product solve?
5. How much will it cost your customer if they don't fix this problem?

Dr. Jim Anderson presents over 100 speeches per year. To invite Dr. Anderson to speak at your event, contact him at:

Phone: 813-418-6970 or
Email: jim@BlueElephantConsulting.com

Blue Elephant Consulting

Speaking. Negotiating. Managing. Marketing.

Chapter 1

What Medical Doctors Can Teach Product Managers

What Medical Doctors Can Teach Product Managers

Once a product has been funded and staffed, there is very little that will cause it to be halted or the original decisions that caused the product to be funded to be revisited. This is probably a good explanation as to why so many products are so poorly received by their intended audience when they finally make it to market. It also explains why product managers have such a hard time getting respect from within their own companies. Maybe it's time to look outside of your product for a better way to do this.

It might seem like a bit of a stretch at first, but the medical profession has been dealing with "bad product development" issues for years. In the world of medicine, the consequences of errors, bad judgments, and flat-out mistakes can be very severe – death. One of the leading causes for these medical mistakes is caused by doctor misdiagnosis. In these cases, a doctor relies on his set of experiences and his limited knowledge to make patient decisions. The fancy name for this type of flawed decision making is **Comparative Ignorance**. What's really interesting here is that we do exactly the same thing – we decide what products to move forward with based more often than not on what we've seen work in the past. For a product like yours, where everything changes so rapidly, it's decisions like this that have a tenancy to result in poor product feature selection or just flat out bad products.

So how have doctors gone about solving this problem? Hospitals convene regular review meetings which are attended by everyone: faculty, nurses, medical students, etc. At these meetings they revisit patient cases that had poor outcomes and they discuss what happened, why it happened, and what can have been done to ensure that it does not happen again. The result of these meetings is that everyone comes to understand that nobody is perfect – we all make mistakes and can learn from others' errors. In the world of product managment, reviews of the formal decision making process are rare. Even our brothers and sisters in Sales have what they call After Action Reviews (AARs) in which they review lost sales opportunities in the hopes of identifying what changes need to be made in order to avoid another sales loss.

Often times a product manager will have a "wrap-up meeting" as a part of the formal product development process. However, since products rarely ever reach an "end", these meetings often never happen. Perhaps if we put our foot down more firmly and held detailed product review meetings at fixed milestones in the launch process, then we'd be able to learn from ourselves and things would be easier the next time around!

Chapter 2

How To Make The Best Product Management Decisions

How To Make The Best Product Management Decisions

Warren Bennis is a smart guy (professor of business administration and chairman of the leadership Institute at the University of Southern California). He's cranked out a book called **Judgment: How Winning Leaders Make Great Calls** and it has a few ideas that really relate to how Product Managers can make better decisions.

It turns out that the ability to make good judgment calls when you are a Product Manager is very important (surprise!) because of the impact on others that all of your decisions make. When do these Product Managers get called on to make judgment calls? Warrne identified of the most common three areas: people, strategy, and what to do in a crises. We see the impacts of people judgments around us at work every day. Technically gifted folks who get put into a product team management role for which they are poorly suited, great team leaders who get bumped up and become paper-pushers, etc. The successes in choosing the right people for the right job gets reflected in how successful the product will be. The mistakes can cause lots of damage and are expensive to replace and to repair.

Strategy judgments are the big ones that can make or break a career. In today's hyperactive product development environment speed is often prized over accuracy. Warren brings up a great product example in his book: Intel. Many folks don't realize this, but Intel got its start in manufacturing and selling memory chips. When the prices in this market started eroding and the Japanese manufacturers started coming on strong, Intel had to make a product judgment call: stay in the memory chip business or move on to something else? Gordon Moore and Andy Grove made the decision to move on (to CPUs) and the rest, as they say, is history. Good judgment call!

Finally, the ability to make good judgment calls in in middle of a crisis. Once again Intel serves as a good IT product example. Back in 1994, as Intel was releasing the latest version of their x86 chip line it was discovered that under certain circumstances it would return the incorrect answer from a math operation. Initially Intel took the engineering road in its response: it did some math and stated that the average user would only see an error once every 27,000 years. However, that didn't sit well with most of their customers and eventually Intel had to offer to refund/replace the defective chips. This initial response was a very, very poor judgment call on Intel's part.

So what can product managers do to make better judgment calls? Warren suggests that we work on improving four areas of our knowledge that are critical to making good judgment calls: self-knowledge, social-network knowledge, organizational knowledge, and stakeholder knowledge. Hmm, sure sounds like aligning the product management organization with the rest of the business would go a long way to making this a reality!

Chapter 3

The 3 Secrets To Creating Good Product Requirements

The 3 Secrets To Creating Good Product Requirements

Requirements – don't we all have a love 'em / hate 'em relationship with them? You can have the best product team in the world, an amazing entrepreneurial spirit, and yet if you screw up the first step in a product launch, the requirements, then you're basically dead in the water. I'll probably take some hits for this next statement: you can also screw up by spending too much time trying to build the perfect requirements for your product. Great – damned if you do, and damned if you don't. What's a hard working product manager to do?

Researchers at the University of Florida have discovered that as much as 80% of the rework that has to be done on a development product has its roots in defects in the product's requirements. What this means is that no matter what development methodology your team is planning on using, one of the largest opportunities for an IT organization to improve the quality of the products that it creates is to find a way to capture requirements correctly.

About 10 years ago I had the opportunity to work with a colleague whom I'll call Neil. Neil was an excellent product manager and his heart was in the right place – he really wanted to do a good job. On the last product that he had worked on the requirements were all screwed up. This time around he swore that things would be better. He not only interviewed his customers as to what they were looking for, it would be more accurate to say that he grilled them. He wrote, rewrote, and rewrote again the product requirements. He also held big meetings where everyone came together and nodded that the requirements were exactly what they were looking for. (You know how this story turns out!) Neil's product was a complete flop. The customer took one look at it and said that they weren't going to use it because it didn't fit with how they did their work. Argh! Neil had done everything classically correctly – what went wrong?

Actually, Neil had screwed up in three major ways that we'll now talk about so that the same fate doesn't befall you. Here are the three secrets that every Product Manager needs to know when it's time to collect product requirements:

The Customer Is Never Right: One of Neil's biggest errors was listening to his customer. What he should have done was to listen to their business processes. Ultimately the role of every product is to solve a problem. If you just listen to the customer's description of the problem, then you may end up creating a solution that doesn't fit in with how they do their work. Instead, take a long, hard look at where the problem fits into their business processes and you just might discover that the correct solution looks nothing like what they described to you.

Good Enough Is Good Enough: You have to draw the line somewhere and stop the requirements gathering process. Neil couldn't do this – he was on a Don Quixote quest to create the perfect all-encompassing product requirements. Instead of thinking of requirements as being written on stone, try thinking about them as having as many layers as an onion. In order to get thing started, you need to have the first complete layer of requirements. You can then refine, refine, and refine some more while the project has already started. Perfection is never attainable and you'll waste a lot of time trying to get there.

Dedication Is Required: All too often product requirements are not "owned" by anyone after they have been created. What this means is that the orphan requirements quickly become almost useless because of product development decisions that get made on an almost daily basis. However, if someone on the product team is given the responsibility of keeping the requirements up-to-date and ensuring that they are a living, breathing document, then they will have value both at the start and the finish of the project.

There you go, 3 simple secrets that can transform how a product manager collects, uses, and manages product requirements. Now if only keeping the product team aligned was so easy...!

Chapter 4

Q: What Comes Before Requirements,
A: ...

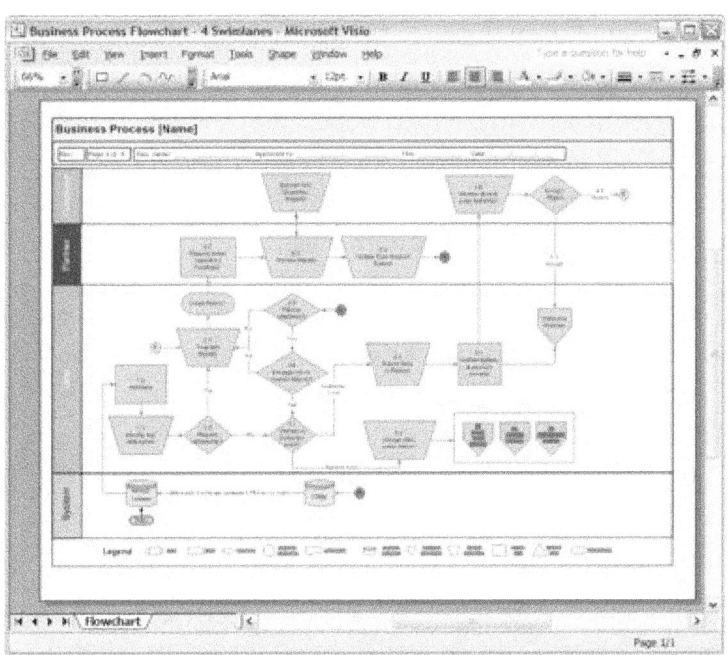

Q: What Comes Before Requirements, A: ...

A good product manager needs to be able to wear many different hats and one of them is that of a Business Analyst. (Oh great I can hear you saying – yet another job for the overworked product manager to take on). Before you throw your hands up in the air and run screaming from the room at being presented with even more work, it turns out that you are already doing this job and just may not know it. I guess we should start our discussion in the beginning – just what is a Business Analyst and why should you care?

We are all familiar with requirements and just how important they are to ensuring that the product that you are working so hard to create meets your customer's needs. What has been missing has been the realization that an analysis of the business needs to be done before any requirements start to be collected. If you don't understand WHAT the business does and, even more importantly, HOW it does it, then there is no way that you'll ever be able to create products that complement the business. All too often Product Managers try to combine the business analysis task with the requirements collection task and end up doing at best half of both jobs.

In some larger companies, there may be whole departments of business analysts, in small firms the full responsibility for this task may fall on the shoulders of the product manager. If we can all agree that the business analyst's role of understanding how the business operates is important, then perhaps we should have a quick discussion to fully understand what a business analyst does?

At a high level, the business analyst is the role that the product manager plays in order to bridge the divide between product development departments and the rest of the business units that they support. No matter if the product being developed is for internal consumption or for external customers, the business analyst's role is to ensure that the most is made of the human contact between multiple internal departments.

The end result of a business analyst's efforts feed into the requirements collection process. However, in order to generate this output, a business analyst needs to start with a clear understanding of what those product requirements will eventually look like. This includes having a good understanding of the plan to eventually create the requirements, what types of requirements will be needed, the process that will be used to gather the requirements, and the planning and preparation that will go into creating the final set of requirements. Note that the business analyst does not need to actually create product requirements; however, they should have a good understanding of what they will look like.

In order to understand how a company does what it does, the business analyst is going to have to do a lot of talking. As the analyst moves from department to department, he/she is going to have to use many different techniques to elicit information from various employees. Some techniques that can be used include:

- Brainstorming
- Job shadowing / observation
- Surveys / interviews / focus groups
- Collaborative work sessions
- Prototyping
- Document / Interface analysis

After having collected all of the information needed to completely describe how the company operates, the next step is to find a way to document this information. As we all know, thick binders of dense text will be put on the shelf and never looked at again. A few issues that the business analyst needs to resolve as the information is processed are:

- Developing Use Cases to show how information & parts move within the company

- Categorizing and packaging the collected information

- Documentation techniques that work best for this particular company / division.

- Change control – critical because of the understanding that process information ages quickly.

In the end the Product Manager / Business Analyst needs to develop and document a detailed understanding of how the company/customer operates in order to prepare to develop product requirements. The skills that a Product Manager needs to have in order to do this successfully are as follows:

1. The ability to elicit and assess information from information holders.

2. The ability to conduct interviews with users and business leaders.

3. The ability to facilitate collaborative sessions.

4. The ability to resolve conflicts and reach consensus.

5. The ability to navigate internal politics.

6. The ability to foster creative problem solving within the various departments.

7. The ability to document the business information that has been gathered.

Chapter 5

Shall We Talk About Product Pricing?

Shall We Talk About Product Pricing?

Have I ever told you just how much I love pricing? In the world of product management, there are so many talented people that I always felt both jealous and just a little overwhelmed. I mean there are product managers who have an amazing depth of product knowledge, there are product managers who know their markets inside and out, and of course there are those product managers who know how to get anything that they want done within their company done and done quickly. How the heck was I ever going to measure up to these gods of the field? It took quite some time; however, I'm pleased to say that I found my niche – pricing.

I discovered pricing somewhat by accident while working for a large European telecommunications equipment provider. Once upon a time, when I had a brief moment to stick my head above the waters of daily product management activities, I realized that none of my peers wanted to touch anything having to do with pricing. All pricing related activity was shoved off onto the finance department from which magical prices would reemerge. In a nutshell, nobody had any clue as to why we priced our products where we did. I didn't take any action on this little nugget of information at the time; however, I started keeping my eyes open.

My next surprise came as I started to get some more insight into how the sales teams were selling the product. The first thing that seemed to go out the door was the list price. After that, it seemed to be a race to see how low we could drop the price in order to get the sale. I was seeing discounts as large as 50-60% on relatively new products. Without knowing any better, I assumed that whatever magic price the folks in finance had set was able to withstand this kind of massive discounting. It turns out that I was wrong.

Collectively as Product Managers, we spend our time on finding ways to capture a larger share of the market all the while increasing customer satisfaction. We've been taught that if we can do these things, then somehow big profits will somehow magically follow. Unfortunately, there never seems to be enough profit magic to go around in the world these days...

Most firms didn't worry all that much about pricing in the past. As long as you knew how much a product cost to make, then you could tack a generous profit margin on top of that and you were set. However, this all changed in the 1980's. This is when the long established market leaders started to get their clocks cleaned by new startups that didn't seem to care about market share. Instead, these new competitors specifically targeted the larger firms most profitable customers (known in the biz as "cream skimming"). This was followed by a wave of companies being taken private, having their product prices raised even as market share dropped and yet still starting to rake in huge profits.

Just as a final confirmation of the importance of pricing and making a profit, need I remind you of the dot.com era? All those new companies went on a footrace to try to build the largest market share, profits be dammed. Ooops, when it all ended the quickest runners went bankrupt while the few that had actually still focused on profits were the last men standing.

I finally had a chance to sit down and talk with some of my friends in the finance department over lunch and I asked about the magical process that they went through to set prices. You can imagine my surprise when I found out that all they were doing was taking the cost of the product, adding the current "company overhead" margin, and then adding a 35% profit margin on top of that with the expectation that it would be discounted no more than 10%. Ouch – talk about simplistic pricing! My friends pointed out to me that the company was more concerned about growing revenue than profits at this time and so that was why I was seeing some fantastic discounts being approved.

Needless to say, this was sorta like discovering that Santa wasn't coming this year. The secret pricing knowledge that I thought that Finance had really wasn't there – the emperor had no clothes! I spent much time after this focusing on learning as much about pricing as I could and that information has served me well over the years. Take the time to research how your company does its pricing and you too can become a master of product pricing.

Chapter 6

Strategic Pricing –
It's About Time!

Strategic Pricing – It's About Time!

Did you ever have a lemonade stand as a kid? If not that, then you probably sold something else at some point in time. When I had my lemonade stand, most of the morning was spent dragging a table to the edge of the yard by the street, creating a hand painted sign that said "Lemonade" and taping it to the table, and then, of course, actually making the lemonade. That was the fun part. Everything was good until my first customer would drop by and ask "how much for a cup of lemonade?" Umm, good question it turned out – I had no idea. I seem to recall that most people would leave me a quarter and some kind souls would drop a dollar in my change cup. The funny thing is that that was a long time ago, but all too often for products the price of the product is the last thing that we product managers think about…!

Here's some new product manager vocabulary for you: "price setting" vs. "strategic pricing". Price setting is what we all do all too often when we've created a product or feature and then all of a sudden someone drops by and asks us "so, what's it going to be sold for?" **Strategic pricing** is what we all really should be doing and it can make all the difference in the world for our company. Strategic pricing is the "special sauce" that explains why two companies with similar market shares and similar technology often earn wildly different profits.

In order to perform strategic pricing, you need to bring together marketing, competitive, and financial information in order to determine how to set prices profitability. Do you see what I'm getting at? This all means that if someone proposes a product or feature that can't be sold at a profit, then you need to kill the product before eats up too many company resources.

So where does all this talk of strategic pricing lead us to? How about a new relationship between marketing and finance. If you think about it, a product's price (and thus the strategic pricing process) is really the interface been a marketing department and a finance department. This means that both sides need to learn some new dance moves. Specifically, marketing needs to come to understand that although market share is important, so to are company profits. Finance needs to learn that pricing is not just about "covering costs", but rather is a part of the dynamic selling process.

Chapter 7

Forget The iPhone: What Can Apple Teach Product Managers?

Forget The iPhone: What Can Apple Teach Product Managers?

Ah, to be a product manager at Apple – working for a company with very good mojo, cool products that everyone wants, and probably a really good bonus program! What more could any of us want? If, for just a moment, we could push the product hype, the speculations about what product Apple will introduce next off to the side and focus on some of the normal day-to-day stuff that we all deal with – but see how Apple product managers handle it.

It always helps if we have a good case study, and what do you know we do: Apple's iPhone 3G power adaptor. The iPhone 3G shipped with a ultra-compact USB adapter that was provided for with all iPhones sold in the U.S., Japan, Canada, Mexico and several other Latin American countries (it looked like pretty much everyone who uses 110V household current). It turns out that its prongs could break off in power outlets and cause a risk of electrical shock to iPhone users. Oh, oh – what's a product manager to do?

The challenge here is that apparently the problem was showing up in *"... a very small percentage of the adapters sold..."* as reported by Apple. Additional, no injuries were reported. Hmm, this is always one of those big product manager moral problems: it looks like it was a *possible problem*; however, it had not really turned into a problem. Just to make things a little bit more interesting, there was a work-around. It turns out that the iPhone 3G can be charged by connecting it to a computer via a USB cable, using a car charger adapter, or even by using a different model of the USB power adapter.

Hmm, which road should a product manager take? This is not like the big Tylenol scare, or even the Intel Pentium math error issue. Instead, it is a possible product issue that has the possibility to either quietly go away or blow up in a product manager's face. W.W.A.D? (What Would Apple Do?)

You've probably already guessed the answer, the Apple product manager(s) decided to exchange the power adapters for new ones without the prong-breaking-off-issue. Here's what their press release said:

> **Customer safety is always Apple's top priority, so it has voluntarily decided to exchange every ultra-compact power adapter for a new, redesigned adapter, free of charge.**

Now how's that for making lemonade out of lemons? Once again, perhaps there is something about taking the high road that we can learn from the product managers at Apple...

Chapter 8

What's A Product Manager To Do When Your Product Is A Service?

What's A Product Manager To Do When Your Product Is A Service?

Pick up just about any Product Management book, thumb through it, and you'll quickly come to realize that most thinking about how to be a successful product manager is based on real products. Things that you can touch and feel. Things that people somewhere in the world manufacture. Even if you are responsible for a software product, there is almost always a set of CDs/DVDs that you deliver to the customer. It's a bit weak, but you can still touch this product. So what's a product manager to do when you CAN'T touch the product – because it's a service. How does this change the product management game?

Before we dive in to this discussion too far, let's take just a moment and ask the question "why sell services in the first place?" If you work for a company that has traditionally sold "hard goods" – things that you can touch, then one of your biggest product manager worries is that your product will eventually become a commodity. When that happens, the only thing that will matter to the customer is your price and I'm going to bet that you probably don't have the lowest price out there. Most firms see selling services as a way to make their hard products unique – provide them with a competitive advantage. The challenge here is that all too often, companies that enter the service space end up struggling to make money – it's not as easy as it looks.

So why is it so hard to start selling services instead of hard goods? A couple of researchers from Europe, Dr. Werner Reinartz and Dr. Wolfgang Ulaga spent some time looking into this and wrote up their findings in the Harvard Business Review.

One of the interesting things that they found was that the back-office automation of services that are complex turned out to be much more difficult than anyone though that they would be. The tendency of customers to want service offerings to be customized for them meant that there really was very little knowledge that could be leveraged across customers.

Another big problem was with the sales teams. They had spent years developing relationships with low-level purchasing staff who were authorized to buy small quantities of hard goods. Once you started talking about selling a service that the whole company could use, the price tag went up dramatically and the sales teams needed to be talking with purchasers who were much higher in the food chain.

Finally, actual knowledge about the new service always seemed to come from "outside" – contractors, consultants, etc. This meant that it was both difficult and time consuming to answer customer's questions. Clearly all of these challenges made it look like the move to selling services is a real pain in the neck. So why even bother?

The answer to that question is simple: once you get beyond the product differentiation issue, it's all about the money. As an example, one group of companies that the good Dr.'s studied was able to get 50% of their sales from services and on those sales they were able to get 8x margins over their hard product sales. That's just too much money to walk away from.

Chapter 9

---

4 Key Success Factors For Being A Service Product Manager

4 Key Success Factors For Being A Service Product Manager

It's hard enough to be a product manager for a "real" product, just imagine how hard this job gets when your company decides to switch over and start to offer service products. You'd think that a flexible product manager could just quickly adjust and that there would be no real difference between managing "hard" products and "service" products. Umm, you'd be wrong.

When your company makes the big decision to move over and start offering service products, your life as a product manager will change big time. There are four key success factors that you will need to make sure that you take care of in order to ensure that you will be a successful product manager for services:

1. **Make The Company Understand That It's Already A Service Company**: Once your company has decided to start offering service products, you may find that you are already doing this.

   Instead of inventing new products, perhaps all you have to do is to start charging for things that you are already doing. As a product manager, your first step here will be to work with your customers to make sure that they are aware of the value of your existing services. You've got to be careful here: when you suddenly switch a service from being free to now charging for it, you've got to make sure that you clearly define the value of the service to both the customer and your internal management.

   The larger your company is, the better the chances are that you already have services hidden somewhere in how you are currently doing business. One of the best ways to uncover what you already have is to take a look at customer bills – often different parts of the company bill for different items and some may already be billing for services.

2. **Transform Your Back Office To Support Services:** Product managers know just how important stable internal processes are to your ability to deliver products consistently. Bad news: when you start to offer service products you are going to find that customer requests to have the service customized to meet their particular needs will have a dramatically bad impact on your cost of delivering the product.

   In order to solve this problem, there are three things that you can do: (1) build a flexible platform for delivering your services and meeting customer needs, (2) monitor the cost of each of your delivery processes in order to spot the most costly, (3) use new technology to implement process improvements as soon as possible. What all of this means is that the product manager needs to stay on top of how service products are being delivered.

3. **Update Your Sales Teams:** This may be the most important thing that you do – find a way to transform your sales force that is comfortable selling "real" products into one that can sell service products.

   One of the most difficult points to get across will be the simple fact that service products take a lot longer to sell and the actual process of selling them is both more complex and strategic. As a product manager it's not your responsibility to make the sales teams change; however, how well they manage the transformation will determine how successful your product is.

   Understand that more often than not, a significant number of your current sales teams will end up leaving the company and will be replaced by new salespeople who better understand how to sell services.

4. **Focus On How Your Customers Do Their Work:** Since a service product is really designed to be used by a customer to make their business run more smoothly, a good product manager now needs to shift his/her focus away from how he/she is delivering the service and start to think about how the customer is going to use the service.

   This is an important difference from how "hard" product companies operate – they normally focus on things like how much the product is used and how many of a given product a customer is using. A service product is really designed to solve a problem for your customer.

   This means that the correct way to measure it's value is to see if it is really solving that problem. Be careful, as a product manager you may find that you have a lack of expertise to determine how to use your product to solve the customer's problems better. This may be a great time to bring in a consultant.

Chapter 10

Product Manager Decision Time: Tell Users "Game Over"?

Product Manager Decision Time: Tell Users "Game Over"?

So here's a little story that caught my attention in the Wall Street Journal the other day. The article was entitled "Microsoft Tries Blackening Screens to Fight Software Piracy in China". The gist of the article went on to say that Microsoft had distributed a Windows XP patch to users who have elected to get automatic updates over the Internet that if they are using a pirated version of Windows turns their backgrounds black and then nags them to switch to a legitimate copy of Windows. What do you think about this tactic – a sound business move or a product management disaster?

Perhaps a few more details on this update are in order. The update does not prevent users from using their PCs. You can change your computer's background from the black setting to whatever you want (like a photo); however, every 60 minutes it will revert back to black. Additionally, messages are posted every so often to the screen that warn the user about using counterfeit software products.

In China, a number of potentially unsuspecting folks are getting zapped by this warning. People who may have purchased a computer that was built by someone who used a counterfeit copy of Windows XP are now being notified that their computers are running counterfeit copies of Windows. Microsoft has done two things to minimize the fallout from all of this. They've lowered the cost of a legit copy of Windows XP to $30 and they will send people a free copy of Windows XP if they send them the physical copy of the counterfeit copy that they were using.

From a product manager's point-of-view, I can understand both sides of this story. Microsoft has a massive problem with counterfeiting. Since they have the most popular operating system out there, everyone wants to have a copy of it. However, at the same point in time, Microsoft generates a great deal of money from other vendors because there are so many copies of its operating system out there. The more people who use Windows, the more valuable Microsoft training and documentation becomes to others. All that being said, Microsoft is always working on the next version of Windows, and it's sure to be an instant hit the day that it is released simply because so many people are already using Windows.

Every product manager wants their product to be a success. However, we also want our company to get paid for the product otherwise the company may not realize just how successful our product has been. If we give away demo or free copies, it's very tempting to add some sort of "kill switch" that can or will disable the product at some point in the future in order to motivate the customer to go out and purchase the real product. The challenge that we have here, is that we can't really control what the customer is going to be doing with our product when this happens. I'm going to guess that more often than not, our product will stop working at just about the worst time imaginable. No matter how much the customer likes our product, they are going to be angry with us because we inconvenienced them.

Additionally, no security solution is going to be perfect. We're going to end up cutting off some legitimate users. Can you imagine how angry they are going to be? Microsoft has not released any statistics; however, you know that they must have gotten hundreds of complaints from legitimate users whose computers started incorrectly telling them that they were using counterfeit copies of Windows XP.

When dealing with a software product, it's always been my feeling that once the product is out there it would be a fool's quest to try to hunt down and stop any counterfeit copies that might have found their way in to use. Instead, I've always felt that making each and every user WANT to be a legitimate user was the way to go. What this meant is that I couldn't just launch a software product, have people purchase it, and then forget about them. Instead, I needed to make the purchase of the product just the start of the relationship. It was my job as a product manager to make my customers want to have a closer relationship with my company.

The real trick to being a successful product manager is to create an ecosystem that your customers want to belong to. What this system consists of will be different for each product; however, some common components may include a user group community and the ongoing discussions that occur there, access to developers / technical experts who can answer even the most detailed questions, access to planned new release schedules and a description of enhancements / new features, invitations to user gatherings, etc.

Ultimately, I think that Microsoft has gotten it wrong again. If they made owning a legitimate version of Windows the passkey into a world of access to privileged information and exceptional customer service, then almost everyone would insist on having a non-counterfeit copy. Having your customers actively avoid counterfeit copies and actually requesting legit copies is the way to go.

Chapter 11

How Dell Product Managers Stole Christmas

How Dell Product Managers Stole Christmas

Q: How can you tell when a Product Manager drops the ball?

A: When there is an article in the Wall Street Journal with the title "As Holidays Approach, Dell Lags In New Products"

Man, talk about having your failures broadcast to the whole world! In the consumer space in which Dell sells some of its PC and notebook computers, the end of the year Christmas holidays are the key to a company's survival. The sales that occur during this time generally account for 30% – 50% of Dell's annual consumer PC revenue. Miss this revenue train and you're going to be standing around waiting for the next opportunity for quite some time!

Where did product managers let Dell down? One place is in an ambitious mini MP3 player that Dell was planning on introducing. Way back in 2007, Dell bought a company called Zing in order to get access to their entertainment software. However, now Dell has decided not to launch this product before the holidays. Ouch! What this means is that the folks who would have bought this product will now go out and buy iPods and, maybe, Zunes. Once they do that, Dell is probably flat out of luck – once you've loaded your iPod up with $200 worth of songs, you sure don't want to change players.

Interestingly enough, Dell product managers are not just falling down in the cutting edge new product area, they also seem to be dropping the ball in their bread & butter areas such as notebooks. So far this season, Dell has only released two netbooks (low end laptops, good for web surfing and emails) and some new paint schemes for some existing notebooks. Remember, they are playing in a highly competitive market – Apple just cranked out that very cool all aluminum Macbook and even Acer has released a bunch of new notebooks computers that have fancy styling and built-in access to 3G networks. What's going on with those Dell product managers?

Michael Tatelman is Dell's retail chief. He has been forced to tell the press that "You'll see some very sexy products coming out of Dell", though they may come out after the holidays. Double ouch!

Way back in the Fall, Michael Dell had told investors that Dell would *"focus on killer products…"* and that they would have a *"shorter development cycle"* that would allow them to get products out *"40% to 50% faster"*. Hmm, missing the Christmas season sure makes it seem like that is not going to happen.

This isn't the first time that the Consumer products division of Dell has missed a great opportunity. Back at the start of the school year they had to hold back on introducing their first netbook because of keyboard problems and so they missed most of the back-to-school selling window. That probably explains why the consumer products division failed to make a profit in the last quarter and why Dell just got done laying off 9,000 of its workers.

What's going on here? As product managers we are all probably quite familiar with the problems that Dell is facing. It sure looks like their new product pipeline, which is the lifeblood of Dell's consumer division, has a friction problem – products are not traveling through it quickly enough. A product manager can't fix a problem like this by his / herself. However, it is our responsibility to get the various folks who can fix it together and knock some heads in order to get it solved. Since this problem has existed since the start of the school year, clearly there is a lingering sense of a lack of momentum at Dell.

What should the Dell product managers be doing? They need to start with a calendar and determine when they need to have new products in order to match up with their customer's buying cycles. Once they have this, then they need to start with with the finished product and work back. What should the next product look like and what features will it have? Once this is nailed down, they need to determine how that product can be available by that date. Very basic stuff, but it sure looks like this is not happening. If a product can't meet a date, then you need to determine what functionally can be dropped to still meet the date. If too much would have to be dropped, then and only then should you start to move dates around.

Dell can recover from these blunders, but it's going to require that their Product Managers step up and take responsibility for fixing the system.

Chapter 12

What Can The Great Scion Teach Product Managers?

What Can The Great Scion Teach Product Managers?

Just in case you have been living at your desk for the past couple of years and hadn't noticed, Toyota launched a new line of cars a few years ago called Scion. Now we all know the Toyota brand – in fact many of you probably own a Camry because it's the most popular car in the world. However, it's a bit on the boring side.

So what's a major world class car company to do when they want to reach out and capture the hearts and minds of the Generation Y drivers who were not currently sitting behind the wheel of a Toyota? Simple: do the unexpected.

As product managers we are often proud of all of the customers that have selected our product. However, deep in our dark hearts we yearn to be selected by all those other buyers who have not yet picked us to go to the dance with them. We often find ourselves in the same situation that Toyota did: trying to make our product appeal to a whole new segment of customers.

Rob Walker has written a book called **Buying In: The Secret Dialogue Between What We Buy and Who We Are** in which he did a lot of studying of just what makes us buy things and he's made some amazing discoveries. One of the things that he learned is that Toyota figured out that in order to market their new car to their Generation Y target audience, the brand's "meaning" was more important than the product's functionality. Can anyone say "iPhone"?

In this highly connected age we've started to believe that our customers have become immune to just about any type of communication that we can come up with. What Toyota's product marketing team discovered was that this was not true. In fact, the pitch-free guerrilla marketing that Toyota engaged in to promote the Scion line actually seemed to be welcomed by their potential customers. Toyota advertised the Scion in small artsy magazines and stayed away from the mainstream ones. They hosted dance parties and gave out Scion CDs and magazines.

What Walker has found out is that the 21st Century "new consumer" is basically all made up. Oh, and this is really starting to screw up product managers. However we do live in changing times and you are going to have to be changing the ways in which you appeal to your customers.

No matter what product you are responsible for, you are going to have to start to emphasize the meaning of the product first and the functionality second (sorry about that feature lovers). Today's buyers want to feel as though they are part of something bigger than themselves ("I'm a Mac").

This goes hand-in-hand with Walker's other finding which shows that successful brands often build their eventual mass audience by cobbling together much smaller ones.

There is a great deal for product managers to learn here even if you are not selling to Generation Y consumers. You need to realize that the world has changed and it's now time to think differently about your customers. They never were nameless, shapeless blobs who mindlessly did or did not select your product. They have always been thinking, caring people for whom your product solved a specific problem. Now you've got to understand how THEY want to be reached...

Hard work does not
guarantee success;
However, success does
not happen
without hard work.

— Dr. Jim Anderson

Create Products Your Customers Want At A Price That They Will Pay!

Dr. Jim Anderson is available to provide training and coaching on the two topics that are the most important to product managers everywhere: how do I create the products that my customers want and what should I price them at?

Dr. Anderson believes that in order to both learn and remember what he says, product managers need to laugh. Each one of his speeches is full of fun and humor so that what he says "sticks" with everyone.

Dr. Anderson's Product Management Training Includes:

1. How can you segment your market?
2. What problems are your customers having right now?
3. Which of your customer's problems does your product solve?
4. How much of this problem does your product solve?
5. How much will it cost your customer if they don't fix this problem?

Dr. Jim Anderson presents over 100 speeches per year. To invite Dr. Anderson to speak at your event, contact him at: **Phone: 813-418-6970 or Email: jim@BlueElephantConsulting.com**

Blue
Elephant
Consulting
Speaking. Negotiating. Managing. Marketing.

Photo Credits:

Chapter 12 – By: The Toad

www.ingramcontent.com/pod-product-compliance
Lightning Source LLC
Chambersburg PA
CBHW071641170526
45166CB00003B/1380